I0151342

Whirlwind, Thorn Tree, Tumbleweed

poems by

Stephen Benz

Finishing Line Press
Georgetown, Kentucky

Whirlwind, Thorn Tree, Tumbleweed

ACKNOWLEDGMENTS

Trailer Park in *New Madrid*
Hopperesque in *Nimrod*
The Cat Hoarder in *Barely South*
Double-A Pitching Change in *Worcester Review*
Broken Main in *Slant*
Weeding the Flowerbeds in *IthacaLit*
Winter Work; Elegy: One Year Since He Died in *Tar River Poetry*
Her Last Wish in *Tule Poetry Review*
Haibun: Bashō's Last Journey in *Portland Review*
Thinking of Du Fu in *Chicago Quarterly Review*
Escape West in *Southwestern American Literature*
Hopi House in *Progenitor*
The Car Runs out of Gas in *El Portal*
Visiting the Asylum in *Burningword*
Starlight in *Naugatuck River Review*
Crossing Flagstaff in *The Sow's Ear Poetry Review*
Night then Morning: Elko Nevada in *Map Literary*
The Desert Mirage in *High Desert Journal*
Across the Great Divide in *Southwestern American Literature*

Publisher: Leah Maines
Editor: Christen Kincaid
Cover Art: Library of Congress, Prints & Photographs Division, FSA/OWI
Collection, LC-DIG-fsa-8b27109
Author Photo: Stephen Benz
Cover Design: Elizabeth Maines McCleavy

Printed in the USA on acid-free paper.
Order online: www.finishinglinepress.com
also available on amazon.com

Author inquiries and mail orders:
Finishing Line Press
P. O. Box 1626
Georgetown, Kentucky 40324
U. S. A.

Table of Contents

Trailer Park

1.
So many enigmas here in Magnolia Gardens:
our dogs are enraged
when a boy spins gravel
with his Sting Ray bicycle.
From each riled property:
yelps and yowls. Snarls.
A Chihuahua behind pink priscillas;
a pit bull yanking on its chain,
forefeet clawing air, spittle flying.
A torn screen door opens
and a bare-bellied man with a rifle
steps from the interior darkness.

2.
Selling school candy
I climbed three metal steps
to the doublewide and rang
an Over-the-Rainbow doorbell.
A woman wearing a yellow kimono
admitted me to the high volume of Another World.
"Just a minute, honey," she said
and pointed me to a ragged La-Z Boy.
"Them chocolates look good,
but I can't miss my show."

3.
On the outskirts of town you find
a row of mobile home dealerships,
an abandoned drive-in theater,
triple X book stores and bars
with "live girls dancing nude."
Then an entrance drive bordered
with plastic geraniums, a sign that says
Residents and Guests Only.

4.
Each day I find new reasons to love the world.
A student asks me to dinner in her trailer home.
"Go ahead take your shoes off, stay a while,"
she says, and I do, placing them on a plastic mat

next to Tinker Bell sandals. The girl is riding
her Strawberry Shortcake tricycle in the drive.
"Tina, you all watch for cars now,"
my student yells out the window.
We eat on trays before the TV console—
venison burgers from a brother's hunting trip.
I rub my soles in the green pile.
"I just loved that poem you read
in class today," she tells me, then aims
at the television and changes channels.

5.
I have a good friend who piously suffers her pains.
She keeps cats, scores of strays
with missing eyes, snipped tails, mange.
Her own ailment is a mystery.
I've watched her give herself cortisone shots
sitting at her vanity in a nightgown,
needle and cigarettes duplicated
in the looking glass, a fierce wind
rocking her '72 Fleetwood,
rattling the roof and spooking
her poor babies, the cats.
"Some days I don't know how
I can go on," she says. "But you do,
you just do, knowing this is what
the Lord has willed for you.
Trust and obey, I tell myself, trust and obey."

6.
There's a low spot where water collects
and stagnates. The county sprays it
for mosquito control. Elsewhere, behind
the back lots, a de facto dump
thick with weeds accepts whatever
is tossed, the broke-down stuff beyond repair
but too big for the bins. Box springs,
consoles, invalid potty, dress mannequin.
It's convenient, we like to say.
Saves a trip to the landfill.
Good place for the kids to catch toads and snakes.

7.
"Look at that light, the setting sun, beautiful,
ain't it? Yes, indeed, very, very beautiful
and this bourbon is good. Real good.
I believe I'll sit here a while
in this lawn chair, young man,
until the light is gone for good.
And maybe, just maybe I'll go on
sitting here for a spell after that.
When you got it this good,
no reason to make a change,
no reason a-tall. Just keep that in mind,
son, and you'll be all right in this old world."

8.
Late at night, alone in my rental unit,
windows open to catch the breeze,
I listen as human sounds fade.
Out in the bog: a ghost owl
repeats his low, deep trill.
I can believe the message has meaning,
but what it is I do not know.

Hopperesque

The inner life of a human being is a vast and varied realm.
—Edward Hopper

1.
Now is the time for nuance,
probing for subtext. She recalls
he once used the word "standstill"
in a letter and she puzzled for days
at the cruel expression of his apathy.
That was before the ill-advised wedding,
before the feckless ocean crossing,
when boredom and close quarters
sapped all compassion. Now she reads
the latest missive for misgivings,
the subtle irony of regret, knowing
of course he will never come clean.

2.
One day there's hell to pay:
simple fact of anyone's life.
The foundation seems solid enough.
Four walls, a good roof,
the furnishings that make for comfort
and ease. But furnishings are also
trappings, and one day you wake up
trapped, whichever way you turn.
Tick, tick, tock. Long ago you colored
at the kitchen table while daddy
finished off the whiskey dregs.
"Son," he said. "You work, you drink,
you die. One day there's hell to pay.
That's all the wisdom your old pop's
got for you." You answered him
the way you were taught: "Yes, sir."
And today, five years older than he was then,
you still don't have a better answer.
You stand in the backyard
as the day goes dark thinking yes, sir,
one day there's hell to pay.

3.
His habit: watching the sea

for hours. No real purpose in it,
just what he must do.
Water. Light. The smell of salt.
The warpage of the porch,
planks absorbing moisture.
It's all about time, the tide
sneaking up, falling back,
shadows in motion,
the day's long journey
passing him by.

4.
Morning after a restless night.
The window admits harsh light,
and he is glad for the brutal glare,
the way each object declares itself
when lit up. Chair, book, bedclothes.
The world of bad dreams
temporarily banished,
a reassurance that *this*—not that
nightmare world—is reality.
All right, he tells himself, *all right.*
That's over for now and I'm still here.

5.
The moment of recognition:
this is the place she cannot escape.
Not even walking through the door
would do the trick, a false threshold.
Light pours uninvited into the room,
cold and daunting, her nakedness exposed.
Shadows are implacable, the books
evoke phantoms. Bedstead. Writing desk.
Drought-stricken trees beyond the pane,
beyond her ken. Well into dotage,
her grandmother had a habit of saying,
"I'm in fine whack, praise God,"
But no such lie will serve, not now, not here,
entrapped as she is, nothing to stave
off the worst of it, the light, these walls.

6.
Dark windows
reveal nothing
of the life inside.
Light can bestow
dimension—
or steal it.
Sudden
luminosity.

7.
It was not the evening of choice,
the theater with its smoky laughter
and maudlin tears.
The particolored curtain
chattering about free fall,
the subtext inscrutable.
The bogus dialogue
that charms bluestockings.
How they pore over
the program in search
of spiritual direction
or gossip or fashion advice.
A moment of darkness
relieves the gloom—
and then limelight
and blare and sulfur—
the pangs intensified,
the rabble uproarious.

8.
In the office
all is official,
files of light
cut corners
angular and true.
Each object holding
and withholding
the magic moment.
Scissors, paste,
typewriter. Above all

the telephone's insistent bell
with the power to summon him
to its court, no recourse.
Is there no way out,
is there no way—
the thought returns
and is again cut short,
filed away. Just like that
another day has fled.

9.
This is the room where hard sunlight
stakes its claim and darkens moods.
This is the book that confounds diligence.
Hard to read with the page so bright
and the air so still. This is the floor
that will not bear weight. Idly pull
a loose thread and now the plot unravels.
The pain that will not let go;
the dread that will not ease up.
This knife-edge of deep shadow
clarifying persistent doubts.

10.
Once again the backlog extends into evening,
all the columns that will not total out,
the correspondence nagging from the inbox.
Nothing alleviates the ambient lighting,
not the radio, not the snippets of small talk—
movie plots and one-day markdowns,
close-out pricing, starlet tells all.
Shooting the breeze as it enters the window
and shuffles the papers, the eight common
fallacies of the modern workplace
all on display in the décor, the attire,
the *mise en scène*. Somewhere beyond
this door a telephone is ringing and ringing.
Will there be an answer? Yes and no. No.

11.
It's a hard road into this place,
and a longer way out. The dark woods,
the lonely storefront, no one
to pump the gas. The moment
for resolution has passed.
Nothing to do but sit and wait
out the gloaming. A dog barks
in the distance. Raccoons scour garbage.
Even a shotgun blast would be welcome.
The next milepost is unknown, far off,
and there won't be a soul for all the trouble.

12.
Motels are for taking stock,
the degradation of surface sheen.
Illuminated objects become a reminder
of the journey's faulty premise.
The window frames a landscape
of uncertainties, the map has more
questions than answers
about the road ahead. It has become
important to linger a moment
on this bed, ignoring for the time being
the suitcase's insistent claim.
The western sky, reflected in mirrors,
promises a hard spell of aimless wandering.
Stationery on the desktop. What would a letter
home say? Who would be there to read it?

13.
Early morning, not yet seven, and already
a desolate atmosphere scarring
the town's main drag. Shuttered storefronts,
wind-blown trash. Obscured messages taped
to window panes. A lone walker on an errand.
What is his cause? Medicine? Milk? The paper?
A dog answers his footsteps with desultory barks,
a gate creaks on its hinges. Doorways recede
deep into shadow, reluctant to let their secrets out.
Dawn without promise; light without glow.

14.
The doctor called it anxiety,
a book said dread. Her friend
shook her head: *just a funk,*
girl, ocean air's what you need.
You'll be right as rain, no time.
Now she's looking out a window:
dunes, sea oats, blue horizon,
that same blunt feeling adrift
on the wind that tousles her hair.
Down on the beach a boat is dead;
gulls cry. She wants to shed her clothes
and all constraint, let sunlight
warm her skin but there's no warmth
here, the light strangely cold.
Fragments of a dream needle her,
and when she hears the words
Lucy, honey, what's wrong,
the prickling of her skin is more
than she can bear. There could be tears,
but there won't be tears, only a plea.
I must make a clean break, I must.

15.
All too abruptly daylight leaves the room.
His prospects for the next few hours:
not good. He's had a dream
but lost the content, whatever stirs
beyond the pane, teasing the edge
of darkness, doesn't want his prayers.
Even the air is nervous, charged,
his skin like paper at the cusp
of flame. All day it's been a slow burn.
He expects the earth to feel dead,
absolutely dead, despite the kinetic dance,
the electric particles, the flare
that startles these window highlights.
There's a ritualistic text—secret
wisdom—to explain this night surge
but the code is lost, the words amount
to nonsense, nothing more, even if

the sound is lovely enough to inspire faith.
Won't such clamor only be futile?
Won't expression quickly pall?
So it goes when the day dies and night
filters into the corridors, the rooms
where novices await insight.

16.
Drink, drank, drunk again—
the various conjugations
of the DTs. And now storms
in the offing, "Stormy Weather"
on the radio, droll cosmic joke.
Crabs on the boil, crustaceans
writhing in a murky sky.
A man gropes in the blue light
of a motel room, hand brushing
objects he can't identify.
Sand blows against the screen
of an unhinged door. Somewhere,
beyond vision, storm clouds
are tossing in their sleep.
The morning mirror reveals
a doped dreamer sloshing about,
the waterline knee-deep and rising.
In motel rooms across the island,
dead-end drummers rifle suitcases
wondering what to wear
for a monsoon season too soon come.
By now the man should know the drill:
it's past time to get his wardrobe out,
ready for the season, his last for sure.
He knows what to do but can't
bring himself to act. Stasis is absolute.

There it is, closer now: the sound,
the smell of the coming rain.

The Cat Hoarder

My mother is at wit's end with her neighbor.

When I come for a visit she says, "Can't you do something, dear—all those cats. And the smell, the filth, the poor woman's gone plumb mad."

From an upstairs window I watch the adjoining lot where cats—at least thirty—loll in the sun of the unkempt yard. One scratches at a pine tree trunk. Three more pace nervously at the patio door, tails erect and twitching. It's a motley collection: tabbies, calicos, and tuxedos. A few torties mixed in.

When I cross the yard—the stink getting stronger with each step—five or six cats scamper off into bushes. Two start up, then freeze in a tense crouch, alert to the threat, ready to run.

Up close, I see mange, missing eyes, bit-off ears, deep wounds oozing and infected. There is mewling and hissing. The dead grass is pocked with crusted piles.

No one answers my knock.

I remember when boyhood home runs crossed this fence, and I'd jump over to fetch the whiffle ball. The grass was thick and green back then, and Mrs. Burke waved brightly from her window. She had maybe two or three cats in those days. But the feline silhouettes decorating her mailbox and welcome mat suggested a fondness, and so the neighborhood came to think of her as a cat lover. When the Glenns moved away they left Rosie with her. The Harwoods gave her a couple of kittens from an unwanted litter. And at least twice we kids brought her the strays we had found, surprised and impressed by her joy and kindness upon taking them in.

"Oh, look at you, yes, just look at you, little kitty, kitty, let's get you some milk, there now you poor hungry thing."

I remember the pathos in her voice as I look through the listings to find the proper agency of city government for handling the matter: Animal Control, according to the blue pages.

While the men in white jumpsuits snatch the cats, their long poles equipped with noose-like loops, Mrs. Burke is bawling and beating her fists against the porch rail, a caterwauling that brings neighbors to their doors.

"Typical case," the lead agent of impoundment tells me. "Old woman, all alone, no one to care, just the cats. She fits the profile to a T. Tragic, really, but far worse for the animals. Most of these will have distemper or leukemia. We'll end up putting them down, I bet."

And then he hands me the clipboard, pointing out the X where I am supposed to sign, confirming the Citizen's Complaint.

Next morning, well before dawn, I am up making coffee. Through the screen I see a beam outside in the darkness. It's Mrs. Burke in bathrobe and slippers, wandering the yard with a flashlight. Just audible above the noise of night insects, she's calling out in a hoarse voice: *Tabatha? Marlene? Henry? Jezebel? Sapphire? Here, kitty, here kitty, kitty.*

Double-A Pitching Change

Maybe a thousand fans in the ballpark tonight, here for diversion,
      escape, baseball's illusion of suspended time. But
      something else is in the air, made manifest late in
      the game: a sudden surge of dread, the old anxiety
      revisiting, a ghost taking possession of the grounds.

It's the top of the seventh, two on, no outs. A graying veteran—
      former all-star in the bigs—is scuffling in his comeback
      bid. He's lost it, can't find the strike zone. Ten straight
      balls—wide, high, in the dirt. The radioman says home
      plate is "jumping around on him."

The pitcher scoops some dirt, rubs the ball, wipes a sleeve
      across his brow, kicks into the rubber, squints toward
      home.

The baby-faced catcher, not long out of high school,
      calls time and trots out to the mound, ignorant of
      the cruel plot now unraveling, blind to all omens—
      the noose in the grass disguised as a groundskeeper's
      hose; the dirge concealed in the organ's carnival tune; the
      unexpected chill that has insinuated itself into the air this
      midsummer's eve.

The pitcher digs and digs with his spiked shoes. The catcher
      chews gum, spits, says nothing.

Now comes the manager's slow stroll, head down, hands
      in back pockets as he makes his way to take the
      ball and, grim-faced, signal for relief. After the
      game he will call the front office to file his report
      recommending waivers.

"Just a shadow of his former self," the radioman says.
      "Sad to see."

The pitcher knows it: he's no longer the ace, the go-to guy, the
      stopper. He's washed up, in the lingo of the boys
      leaning on the dugout railing, a has-been about
      to leave the field for good. This is it, the long
      last walk, ghost-escorted, from mound to dugout

before a scattered and indifferent crowd.

Before he descends the steps, the pitcher takes a final look around
the ballpark. The outfielders are stretching hamstrings,
pounding mitts, impatient to get on with it. The
mascot, freighted with a bulbous head, reels
along the catwalk, seemingly stoned.

Scorecard fanatics diligently line out the pitcher's name and
pencil in his replacement. In the bleachers a lone man
repeats and repeats a hapless gesture: jumping from his
seat, flinging arms above his head.

The pitcher gazes into the night sky past the light standards,
the humming sodium lamps, the moths swimming
in cigarette haze: high in the purified twilight a shooting
star flares and burns out. He is the only one to see it.

At last he brings himself to look out to the bullpen where the
gate opens and a live-armed kid, a promising
prospect, comes sprinting across the grass and dirt to
take his place.

The old pitcher tips his cap to desultory applause and
apathetic jeers. He descends the steps, passes
down the row of silent, stone-faced teammates,
and crosses the threshold into darkness.

Then the tunnel, the locker room, the cage he must clean
out before the final bus ride home.

Broken Main

Someone from Taft Hall calls it in:
flooded grass, stranded cars.
More trouble with the water main.
Every week, the old iron pipe
rusts through somewhere and bursts,
swamping campus lawns and parking lots.

Same old, same old, says the boss
when we reach the scene, three of us
squeezed onto the truck's bench seat,
staring at the task ahead.
Water bubbles from a spring hole
and spills down the sidewalk.
Lot A has turned into a small lake.

Years ago it was all play time,
splashing around in pools like this.
With the blackbirds I looked for worms;
then an afternoon at the creek
waiting for fish to bite.
Now sloshing is part of the job.

Turn off the main, drive down to the shop,
wait for the water to recede a bit.
Lunch and Paul Harvey on the radio
until the boss says, *Max and Stephens
get on up there, dig us a hole.*

With each shovelful, water sucks back in.
Boots soak through, feet prune up.

An hour later, our little triad stares down
at exposed pipe, a six-inch split.
Max kneels in the muck to work the hacksaw.
The boss heads back to the shop to fetch some parts.
People watch our work from office windows,
sipping coffee, looking cool in air conditioning.
One suit grins and gives the thumbs-up.

We're still at it when the secretaries
leave for the day. The boss doffs his hat

and says *Ma'am* as they pass.
We watch them mince down the sidewalk,
gingerly picking a path around puddles.
The prettiest one slips off her shoes
and tiptoes barefoot to an islanded Mustang—
a real beauty, one slick ride.

Come on now, the boss says,
no looking at the ladies.
We got work to do.

Another four hours and
the busted pipe's replaced,
the hole refilled, the lawn spruced up.
The summer sun has already set.

Turning on the main again, we know
the next weak spot down the line
will start to feel the pressure,
ready to burst. Give it a week
and we'll find out where.

Weeding the Flowerbeds

Break time in the shop, the hell-fire space heater
cranked full blast and Paul Harvey's smug voice
on the righteous radio rehearsing the misdeeds of mankind
but promising a redemptive tale, a heartwarming
happy ending right after important messages.

The boss turns on you to say, *Break time done,*
get on up to the Gates and weed them flowerbeds.
It's his Biblical voice, the same one he uses
for reading out loud from the prophets,
and he's giving you the mean deacon look again,
the one that says you've been asleep in the pew
and shirking the Lord's work.
Wake up, sinner, and get on out there
with that scuffle hoe, them weeds don't sleep.

What is the rest of Paul Harvey's story?
You'll never know because you're out the door,
stiff joints and soiled jeans,
the wind a steady gale mocking spring.
And here's your chore for the day,
a choked-up garden along the entrance drive,
long called the Gates of Eden in campus lore,
entryway to the life of the mind—
but for you a dreary, laborious place
where spring's cold showers
have fed the haughty weeds,
and for hours on end you're down
on your knees in mud,
troweling up Creation's bad seeds.

Winter Work

On the coldest days
we stayed in the shop overlong,
our break lasting a full hour
while our feet thawed
and snowmelt from our duds puddled
the weathered and grease-stained boards.
The boss read the Bible, pausing over words
that troubled his brief schooling.
Suddenly overcome with the Word,
he would turn on us and recite:
Where, oh where is wisdom found?
Man do not know. Repeat: Man do not know.
You boys hearken to Job, you hear?
And he gave us the hardest glare
an old army sergeant could muster.
We met him with sighs then silence,
young men aching to knock off for the day
and forget about work for a while.
The lull was all too brief. We hoped for reprieve
but knew in our bones what was coming: He stood
and lumbered on arthritic, war-worn knees;
the door opened to a bone-chilling gust.
Already new snow filled the walks we had cleared.
The boss put on his gloves, saying, *Boys,*
that snow sure ain't going to shovel itself.

Elegy: One Year Since He Died

I've carted the last of the leaves to the pile.
The quad is raked clean.
The air is damp, misty and cold.
Across campus, the lights
in Administration flicker and glow.
There are rumors of more budget cuts,
furloughs, layoffs. Memos tell us
we must do more with less.
All the way back to the shop,
the wheelbarrow rattles and squeals.

Just last year, the old man guided me
through these chores. We worked together,
while the rain beat down and glossed
the yellow leaves. Once, he waved me over
to see what his rake had discovered:
a colony of small white mushrooms.

His lessons were always the same:
There's a right way and a wrong way;
Everything has its time and place;
Don't sweat what you can't control.
I know just what he would say these days:
The Lord giveth and the Lord taketh away.
Behind his back I scoffed
and longed to quit the job I loathed.

Now he's been gone a year.
On the service road behind Taft Hall
I look off into the woods and see a doe
staring me down, stock-still.
At the storage shed just like he taught me
I return my tools to their rightful places.

Her Last Wish

For years I heard
her neighborly stories
of the old homestead,
six states away,
seven decades past.
In her telling,
the place was a glory,
God's country,
the Land of Canaan.
I attended patiently,
and for that she charged me—
a neighbor by chance,
the last person she could turn to—
with fulfilling her most ardent wish,
a charge that surprised
and confounded me, but yes,
I said, I'd do as she asked.

Now, pushing aside weeds,
I have to imagine the wisteria
she remembered climbing
her mother's trellises
toward the piedmont sky.
Here is the remnant
of the slaughter shed where
she saw her first lamb die.
And there's the foundation
of the house from whose window
she watched when older brothers
trudged to the barn and chores.
A few rotting posts mark the old corral.
I cross a streambed now dry
where children once caught
guppies and minnows.

An hour's searching brings me
to the place she mentioned most:
a restful meadow on a hilltop,
where I recite the words
she gave me from Isaiah—
mountains break forth into singing,
trees clap their hands—
and I cast her ashes to the wind.

Haibun: Bashō's Last Journey

*I have always been drawn by wind-blown clouds
into dreams of a lifetime of wandering. –Bashō*

Late autumn, a day of mist and rain keeping me indoors. I think of Bashō at the outset of his final journey: taking up the walking stick, crossing the threshold. All day long I have sat by the window watching rain, reading *The Narrow Road*, strumming the guitar. Outside, dead leaves have piled up, vines have lost their bloom. In a nearby field, cranes pick through harvest remains without concern for the downpour.

Filled with sadness, Bashō's friends watch him go, a sere leaf skittering in bone-chilling wind toward the vanishing point. He must undertake this pilgrimage on his own. Wilderness, mountain pass, desolate shore: the walking stick guides him past all hazards. The haiku brush enlightens his path; he leaves poems pinned to mileposts as he goes.

It has been a long time since I ventured beyond the horizon. Sometimes like Bashō I study maps, plotting routes to the remote interior. Daydreaming, ignoring chores, I conjure the bright moon rising over a mountain lake, the taste of strange spices, the music of an unknown tongue.

"Thousands of miles rush through my thoughts," the poet says. The narrow road has taught him about hardship, the inevitable travails in travel. Some have died mid-journey—Saigyō, Du Fu. This, he knows, is the wayfarer's fate. Steeling himself for the unknown, he crosses another barrier, enters a new province. A crow watches him from a bare branch.

He himself has been a bird flying toward clouds, a horse ever seeking the true path, a boat chasing the horizon. Now, after months on the road, it has come to this: He is stranded in a woebegone inn. Hard rain. A restless night. Far from home, taken ill, he ponders his *jisei*, the death poem: *On a journey ailing—my dreams wander over a desolate moor.*

Night has fallen. I close the book on another aimless day.

*Dusk: rain becomes snow.
On the winter road ahead
there will be no guide.*

Thinking about Du Fu before the Start of a Journey

Why am I loathe to set out
this autumn morning?

Red clouds, fiery sky
to the east and south.

Is it departure I dread,
the impending journey?

Cranes by the thousands
rise up from marshes;

snow geese are loud
with the urge to leave,

flight for them inborn,
a purposeful act.

They fly off with ease
toward warmer skies,

but for me the first mile
is daunting and cold.

Escape West

A cold spring. Week after week of raw winds,
dreary rain. Yards turn to mud, drains back up,
and icy water pools in suburban streets,
slush splashing the underbellies of cars
that try to slog through. Blackbirds wade the yard
snatching up waterlogged worms. Squirrels pause
on window-level branches, gaze in, then vanish
like a name you know but can't quite recall.
You reread *Grapes of Wrath* and *On the Road*,
drinking too much coffee and chafing at the thought
of another hard week at work followed
by dull evenings at home with the television on.
Day by day you watch from safe confines
while the rain streams down. You have a steady paycheck,
a house, some version of the American dream;
but the code of rain tapping the glass tells you to leave,
to hit the open road. Then one morning
the sun breaks through and you find yourself
filling the tank, stacking maps on the dash,
driving away to Dylan on the tape deck,
a drifter's escape. Why this urge to leave,
to make a clean getaway? The morning
shadows are long and leaning westward.

Haibun: The Road West

An all-American freeway, westbound. The urban blight of the rust belt soon gives way to suburban sprawl. Then come the rolling hills of the Midwest, then the vast expanse of prairie, or what used to be prairie before it was plowed under. You cross the Mississippi River and then the Missouri, picking up speed as population dwindles with the rainfall and the road ahead empties. Beyond the 100th meridian lies True West, a land with too little rain for profitable agriculture and a lingering aura of lawlessness. Ranchland replaces the farm belt. The tidy burgs of Middle America yield to tank towns and unincorporated hamlets. Cattle roam the vast fenced-in tracts, while pronghorns and prairie dogs prevail in the open range and coyotes prowl the fence lines. The highway pushes hard toward Wyoming and that elusive promise of unbridled freedom that the West represents. Finally, the frontier is in sight.

A sign up ahead:
Welcome to Wyoming
Forever West

Hopi House

There's nothing left of Hopi House,
rest stop for the road-weary,
ten miles west of Winslow on old Route 66.
The diner served up hotcakes and sausage links.
Cowboy music played on a radiant jukebox.
My brother colored the paper placemat.
Outside, snow flurries rode the winter wind.

There's nothing left of the filling station, the motel,
the adobe façade painted with kachinas and thunderbirds,
Hopi women working looms and carrying pots on their heads.
My father waited with the car at the Texaco pumps
while a gas jockey in cap and bow tie checked oil, air, and water.

There's nothing left of the trading post, the curiosities
and wonders within—Navajo rugs, mineral rocks,
petrified wood, a chance to see rattlesnakes under glass.
My mother searched her purse for coins
and let us choose one souvenir each.
Whatever happened to that old arrowhead?

There's nothing left of Hopi House, nothing at all.
I stood at the crossroads where it used to be.
The wind blew hard, a chill in the high desert air.
The sacred mountain wavered in a gritty haze.
Tumbleweeds skittered across the highway.
A raven lit on a rock to let me know:
there's nothing left, nothing left, nothing at all.

The Car Runs out of Gas, and Mom Says I Told You So

As usual we're cruising right along.
Pop fools with the radio dial
while mom reads the signs:
Almost There! Ten Miles Ahead!
Whether ten or a hundred pop doesn't care.
We're in it for the long haul, he says,
moving out and moving on.
The road goes on forever and it's a free ride.

Rest Area. Scenic View.

Pop scoffs: Who needs rest? What's to see?

Inertia has us in its thrall, no stopping now.

A change of time zones, a change of stations,
"Today's Top Hits" fading
to "Golden Oldies Magic 99."
Rambling man, king of the road, born to run;
Come on now, sing along, you know
the words to this one, don't you, boys?

Here It Is! Don't Miss It!

No Services Next 100 Miles.

Keep on trucking—that's pop's motto.
What are you talking about, there's half a tank.
We'll fill'er up when we cross the line.
Pop's got a hunch it's cheaper over there.

Last Chance Gas.

This is it. Exit Now.

In a blink we've passed it,
certain there's no need;
and the road ahead vanishes

into a shimmering mirage—
pop's boundless dreamland
where nothing can ever go wrong.

Visiting the Asylum

Noises outside: the beating of wings,
a persistent caw, caw, caw.
From the window I see
the evening sun—bloody
through the branches of a dead tree,
a crow perched near the top,
a groundskeeper crossing the leaf-filled lawn.

What did I expect to learn,
making this pilgrimage
just to visit his former room?

There's passing chatter in the corridor,
the clacking wheels of a cart.
Somewhere a phone rings and rings,
a door clicks shut, footsteps fade.

Did he, too, hear the bird's mockery?
Did it foretell renewed anxieties,
the advent of the crisis moment?
Did he stumble to this pane,
peering through the mist
of breath on glass, wondering
who called his name?

I imagine the anguish
when desperate for an answer
from God he gazed
upon this hysterical crow
and the black-garbed groundskeeper
now steadfastly lowering the flag.

Haibun: Antelope Island

A storm in the small hours—thunder, lightning, hail. I woke and listened in the dark to the snapping of ice pellets on tent fabric, and I thought about the many times we had camped in bad weather just like this (waiting out a storm, bundled in the down bag, warming each other until the storm passed) then left the tent for the weak light of dawn, hailstones everywhere spotting the bleak terrain, like thousands of hummingbird eggs. I crunched over them, wiped them from the table, prepped the stove, set a pot on the flame, thinking how much on these trips you loved to wake up to hot coffee, pine trees, mountains, lakeshore, campfire. How on those sacramental occasions you held the cup in both hands, held it to your face, breathing in the steam and quoting Blake: *For everything that lives is holy, life delights in life.* While the water swirled and bubbled toward boil, I gazed at the Great Salt Lake, silver and gray in the dawn. The storm seemed to intensify the sulfur smell. Birds were in flight against the overcast sky. Others waded the shore. Waterfowl of various kinds. You, the bird lover, would know their names; on our journeys I relished hearing you recite the litany of species: avocets, plovers, and stilts. On the hill above the campground a few shaggy strays from the island's bison herd loped in yellow light and snorted, their breath visible, steam rising from their flanks. I thought I heard you sigh and hum a little as you liked to do upon waking, and so I poured hot water over the coffee grounds and got out the cup with your name on it. Distant thunder rattled and grumbled. The bison paused, alert to something, some imperceptible shift in—in what? Air pressure? Tectonic plates? The life force? When the coffee was ready, I imagined your delight, the simple pleasure you would take from the first sip, the cup lingering at your lips. The lake was now luminous—light from some hidden source—and birds were crying out. I felt a chill, unzipped the flap, crawled back into the tent, and wrapped myself in the empty bag, wondering as always about the journey you've taken, wherever you are, wherever you're bound.

> *After the ice storm,*
> *after we have fallen silent,*
> *birdsong goes on.*

Starlight

Nightfall caught me on the edge
of some town; I no longer remember
its name or even the state,
but I do remember the movie complex—
the Starlite 8—and the open space
adjacent to the parking lot
with a little pond, shade trees, and a bench.
Good place to pass the night:
close to the highway but hidden,
little chance I'd be spotted or hassled
(the small town cops being hard
on drifters). I left my pack and bedroll
by a tree then sat awhile on the grassy verge
looking up at the violet neon sign
lighting up one letter at a time.
S-T-A-R-L-I-T-E-8, the whole name
blinking three times before the spelling
exercise started again. Then the show let out.
A teenaged crowd spilled through the lot
where parents waited in cars. A few boys,
new to driving, jangled keys and smirked.
A young couple wandered my way
and I receded into shadow, like the wolf spider
I'd watched one day in a rest area
as it dropped into its burrow each time
I dragged a stick nearby. They stood
close, silent for some time, and peered
into the pond. In a low voice he said,
"I just don't think we'll get away with it."
And she: "It's like the cartoon says,
it's so crazy it just might work."
For a while we listened to cars
driving off. Crickets filled the void.
Then he kissed the top of her head
saying, "All right, let's give it a try."
And they strolled back to the parking lot,
his hands in his pockets, her arms folded
across her chest, clutching herself.
Their footsteps faded. The neon marquee
went dark. Lying on the bench,
rucksack for a pillow, I watched Orion

the Hunter climb and cross the night sky,
blazing Sirius, the ever-faithful
dog star, trailing at his heels.

Crossing Flagstaff

Snow fell that morning as I trudged into Flagstaff.
Snow on snow, more snow than I had ever seen.
There must be some place open up ahead,
I thought—café, tavern, railway depot. But no,
nothing, the entire town shuttered tight.
Icicles daggered down from the depot's eaves,
and a murder's eyes studied me from window wells
when I paused. *Move on,* they cawed, *move on.*
I took it as the gospel truth and followed
Santa Fe, the Avenue of Holy Faith,
pressing onward into wind and whiteout,
the streets empty, storefronts lost behind piles,
the hobo camp buried, wiser vagrants than I
having skipped town for the season.
Halting beneath a blinded street sign,
I understood: This is how it is going to be.
The snow will fall and go on falling,
and I will keep on, crossing one Flagstaff
after another, kicking through drifts
the length of my days.

Haibun: At a Crossroads

Farson, Wyoming, a crossroads point. The junction of two blue highways—a four-way stop sign. Which way to go? North to Yellowstone. South to Rock Springs. Straight ahead for Idaho. Different roads, different directions, a different version of me pursuing alternatives. For a long moment I linger in indecision until an oversized pickup truck comes up from behind. In the rear view, there's a young man already exasperated—no, pissed—before he has even come to a complete stop. He prods with his horn. His lips shape the word "asshole."

And so I'm forced off the road into a gravel lot. Which turns out to be the parking area for a small café, the Oregon Trail Café, with a sign in the window praising homemade pie. Well, that makes it easy: There's always time for coffee and pie—an opportunity to linger in Farson for a bit and put off decision-making.

Inside the Oregon Trail Café, I sit in a booth and take stock: old calendars on the wall. Rodeo posters in the window. Trays stacked on a table. Three women seated, folding paper napkins around groupings of silverware. A row of pies on the counter. A percolating coffee pot. A coat rack with two pairs of muddy boots at its base. A mop in a bucket. A newspaper from last week with a headline about school budget cuts. Two pompoms on a lunch counter stool. Framed photographs of high school basketball teams. Reflective stars glued to the ceiling. A trucker's magazine left behind in a booth. Boxes of pancake mix. Tucked under the sugar dispenser: a crumpled napkin, which opens up to reveal the words *Cowboy, take me away* written with a pink pen. Just another of the many enigmatic messages I keep encountering in my travels.

> *Now the deciding point.*
> *At the crossroads, a hard wind.*
> *Leaves skitter westward.*

Night, then Morning: Elko, Nevada

A late night arrival in Elko, Nevada means no vacancy except in cheap dives like the Louis Motel on the far west end of town. At night, Elko seems rather joyless, even though the billboards on the approach to town promise good times in the form of casinos, brothels, and bars. The point is underscored by a song playing in the Horseshoe Club: "You're supposed to be feeling good…." But in the town's joyspots, there's no evidence of good feelings, not on this night. Tonight, Elko is ground zero in a vast dislocated landscape, the place Emerson called "unapproachable America."

The bars are hazy and rank, with a lineup of men drinking hard and quick, their loud talk lapsing into expressions of resignation: *Yeah, but what you gonna do? That's the way it always goes. Same old, same old.* Around the corner, a gun shop sells "tactical survival" supplies. Just down the street, neon signs flicker in the desert night: the town's three brothels all in a row. Ghostlike in the glow, patrons pass in and out of a shabby door with squealing hinges. In the casinos, people play fast, pumping in money, mesmerized by slot machines or the numbers flashing on the keno board.

In the light of day, Elko tries to strike an upbeat note. After all, it's the home of LeeAnne's Floral Design, Haley's Fine Gifts, the Miss Elko Scholarship Foundation, and a storefront Wedding Chapel. And there's a bargain breakfast in the coffee shop of the Commercial Casino, two eggs any style, toast, and your choice of sausage or bacon. A cup of coffee and things look a little brighter.

But for all that, it's not long before Elko's medley shifts to the minor key, the downbeat. Two elderly folks in a booth are discussing their gambling successes and failures loud enough for all to hear. She's losing heavily, it seems, and he says, "I told you, stop drawing to fill straights—it ain't gonna happen. Play for three of a kind and pairs and you might—repeat, *might*—come out ahead."

The waitresses, meanwhile, carry on their own conversation. "Feels like 11:30," one says. "Wish it was," her partner answers. Then some gossip: "You see that guy in here about six? Drunk and dropping money all over the floor? Thought he'd pass out right in his omelet."

In Elko, cigarette smoke and prosthetics are prevalent. People are not healthy. Everyone in the coffee shop is smoking, except for the guy wheeling around an oxygen tank, plastic tubes hooked to his nose. Another woman has a tube stuck in her throat. There are people with back braces, walkers, canes. Almost everyone looks decrepit; even guys in their twenties and thirties talk in old and weary voices, their shoulders slumped. Or is it just that it's early morning in a casino and what do you expect?

A trucker type comes in, takes a stool at the far end next to another trucker. The newcomer is a little too neat compared to most drivers—Vince Lombardi glasses, pressed jeans, shiny boots—and what's more he's a regular chatterbox. Goes on and on about the trucking business, tossing out buzzwords and trade talk: burning oil, liability, off-loading, air cylinders, hydraulic cylinders. His grittier and more taciturn interlocutor nods, blows cigarette smoke, and grimaces when the stranger pulls out a catalog of trucking supplies: another goddam salesman.

Pouring coffee, the waitress says, "Been winning?"

The question is directed at a young man with a faraway look. He chews his toast slowly, takes his time answering. "Not a player," he says, finally.

"I am," she says. "But I play too much. Some days I put all my tip money in, and that ain't good."

Across the coffee shop, a man gets up from a booth and says to his partners, "I lost it all, now I got to go back and start all over again."

They all laugh, another instance of the weird joviality about losing that predominates in these casino towns. People seem to regard their losses as inevitable, part of the fun they're supposed to be having.

A new arrival now engages the waitress. "Thought you'd be long gone from this place by now, baby doll."

"Nope. Just hanging on."

"Me, too. I keep trying to leave this place and I can't seem to make my break."

"Yeah, they keep me hanging around. Just to see what I'll do next, I guess."

"It's like the goddamned circus."

Time to move on. At the edge of town, Old Highway 40 seems to disappear into heat mirage and a vast searing sky. You're gaining speed, lifting off the cracked and ridged macadam—and it's like you're flying, flying into the great wide open and still not getting anywhere.

The Desert Mirage
after Bashō

You know the tedium and foreboding
that you feel on a long haul
in a wasteland with place names
like Bauxite, Gravemound, Wormwood,
Coffinville, Hangman's Creek.
It's the land of the lost and you best turn back.

But if you don't you will find yourself
drowsy at the wheel—too tired to travel on.
And you stop at a woebegone motel—
the Desert Mirage—a dim bulb, broken screens,
sagging bed, rust stains in the sink,
bad landscapes nailed to the walls.
You fall asleep to gurgling pipes,
neon nervousness backlighting the blinds,
scorpions scratching the concrete floor—
only to be roused in the small hours
by muffled voices through the wall:
two women, a drunk man, now laughing,
now arguing, now singing,
the words momentarily clear:
time makes you bolder even children
get older and I'm getting older, too.

Fate, fate, fate—the inescapable mantra.

Morning in the coffee shop.
You've had a bitter cup, dry toast.
The women show up—sullen, looks like
they've slept in their clothes.
In the parking lot, infernal wind kicking up,
they ask for a ride to Reno.
You've got excuses to put them off:
a roundabout route, just taking it slow,
friends to stop and see. One moment they are girlish,
touching your arm. The next they are pouty and hurt,
another song on bruised lips: *Set me free,* they sing.
Take me away into the wild blue. All day long,
crossing playas and sinks in a white hot glare,
you think about it, the tune stuck in your head. All day.
That evening just before Reno
you see the moon rising over alfalfa fields.

Across the Great Divide

Invoke a state's name,
one of the Western states,
and wander toward it.
The quest requires
a roundabout route,
meandering, slow.
The discourse of magpies
will prompt doubt.
Carrion crows
will offer unwanted advice.
See how the pronghorns
keep their distance?
They understand,
having learned the boundaries,
the meaning of the great divide.

Upon arrival,
there might be a tavern,
Buckhorn Beer in metal cans,
a jackalope nailed to the wall.
The whiskey labels are unfamiliar,
and a rose dripping blood
from its thorns adorns
the barmaid's neck.
But something is missing
from the mythology
that kickstarted this
haphazard journey:
what necessitates escape?
The sober reality—
there is no purpose
to this flight. It's like
witnessing a train wreck
from inside the boxcar,
tossed about, a free fall.

What'll you have, stranger?
the barmaid asks in scripted voice.
And you don't have an answer
except *whirlwind, thorn tree, tumbleweed.*

www.ingramcontent.com/pod-product-compliance
Lightning Source LLC
LaVergne TN
LVHW051610080426
835510LV00020B/3218